D0593730

The Little Book of
Hanukkah

The Little Book of
Hanukkah

Illustrated by Marco Ventura

RUNNING PRESS
PHILADELPHIA · LONDON

A Running Press® Miniature Edition™
© 2000 by Running Press
Illustrations © 2000 Marco Ventura
All rights reserved under the Pan-American
and International Copyright Conventions
Printed in China

Library of Congress Cataloging-in-Publication Number 00-131315

ISBN 0-7624-0790-5

This book may be ordered by mail from the publisher.
Please include $1.00 for postage and handling.
But try your bookstore first!

Running Press Book Publishers
125 South Twenty-second Street
Philadelphia, Pennsylvania 19103-4399

Visit us on the web!
www.runningpress.com

Contents

Festival of Lights

Tradition and the Menorah

Hanukkah has been, for 2000 years, a triumphant expression of the Jewish will to live in freedom.

Chaim Raphael
American writer

As long as Hanukkah is studied and remembered, Jews will not surrender to the night. The proper response, as Hanukkah teaches, is not to curse the darkness but to light a candle.

Irving Greenberg
American rabbi

The **Festival** of **Lights**

Hanukkah celebrates the freedom won from the pagan King Antiochus and his formidable army by a small band of Jews called the Maccabees.

Hanukkah celebrates the
purification and dedication of
the defiled temple in Jerusalem
and the restoration of its
service to God in 164 B.C.E.
"Hanukkah" means
"dedication" in Hebrew.

Festival of **Lights**

Hanukkah falls on the
twenty-fifth day of the third
month of Jewish calendar,
the month known as Kislev,
because this is the day in
164 B.C.E. when the Maccabees
rededicated the Holy Temple.

In the depth of winter, for eight straight evenings, the entire family gathers to light candles of hope.

Rabbi Morris N. Kertzer (1910–1983)
American rabbi

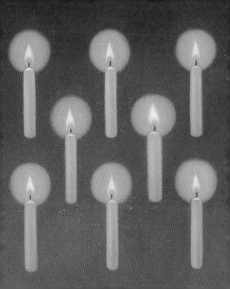

Hanukkah was a very exciting holiday. I did not get to light a candle each night because we had more children than there were candles, but there was always a race to see which candle would last the longest.

Rae Gindi
American pyschotherapist

Hanukkah's symbols are
the menorah, candles,
the Star of David,
the dreidel, the hammer
(Judah Maccabee's sign),
and the elephant
(the animal used by the
Syrian army
under Antiochus).

The Little Book of **Hanukkah**

Menorah is the Hebrew word for "candelabrum." Its nine-branched shape has become the primary symbol for Hanukkah. Eight candles represent the miracle of the oil that burned for eight days. The ninth candle, called the *shamash*, or "servant," is used to light the others. It represents the Messiah and should be set apart by being higher, lower, or farther away from the rest of the candles.

On Friday, the menorah is lit 18 minutes before sundown, before the Sabbath candles are lit.

More rules for lighting the menorah:

Hanukkah candles must burn
for at least thirty minutes.

✡

Candles are placed in the menorah
from right to left,
but they are lit from left to right.

✡

The candles should not be
extinguished, but should
be left to burn out by themselves.

The miracle and salvation
of Hanukkah were a result of the
actions of Jewish women.
Therefore, for at least half an
hour after the flames of
the menorah are kindled, women
should not engage in work.

The Laws of Hanukkah

Everyone in the family
helps light the menorah.
The perfect place for it is
in a front window, so that
the light is shared with
neighbors, too. Traditionally,
the menorah sits to the
left of the doorway upon
entering the house.

On the first night of Hanukkah,
three blessings are said over the light:
l'hadlik ner shel Hanukkah
(to light the Hanukkah candle);
she'asah nissim (who performed
miracles for our fathers in those days
and at this time); and *sheheheyanu.*
For the rest of the holiday,
only the first two blessings are said.

Irving Greenberg
American rabbi

First Blessing

Barukh atah adonai, elohaynu
*   melekh ha-olam*
Asher kidishanu b'mitzvo-tav
Vi-tzivahnu le-hadlikh ner shel
*   Hanukkah*

Praised are You, Oh Lord, our God,
King of the universe,
Who has made us holy through
His commandments and commanded
    us to kindle the Hanukkah lights.

Second Blessing

Barukh atah adonai, elohaynu
  melekh ha-olam
She-asah nisim l'voteynu, ba-yamim
  ha-hem, ba-zman ha-zeh

Praised are You, Oh Lord, our God,
King of the Universe,
Who performed miracles for our
  ancestors in ancient times at
  this season.

Third Blessing

Barukh atah adonai, elohaynu
melekh ha-olam
She-hekhiyanu, v'kiyimanu,
v'higiyanu laz-man hazeh

Praised are You, Oh Lord, our God,
King of the Universe,
Who has kept us alive and sustained
  us, and enabled us to reach this season.

✡ **read only on the first night**

Blessings are our own
voices clothed in the words
of the soul. They call
our attention to spiritually
dramatic moments
that often vanish without
anyone taking notice.

Shimon Apisdorf
American writer

We light candles in testament that faith makes miracles possible.

Nachum Braverman
American writer

Hanukkah Stories

Stories

A Maccabee Primer

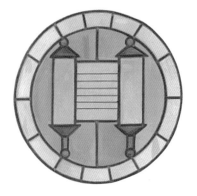

The Rise of
King Antiochus

The miracle of Hanukkah began almost twenty-one centuries ago when most of the Middle East was under the influence of Greek culture. At first, that didn't seem so bad: the Greeks developed architecture and art, they appreciated philosophy and literature, and they enjoyed sports and leisure.

Because the Greeks had so much
to offer, most countries in the
Middle East gladly adopted their
ways. Soon the people of these
countries forgot the ways of their
ancestors. They began to dress like
the Greeks, build their buildings in
the style of the Greeks, speak the
Greek language, and even worship
the Greek gods. The hodgepodge
of cultures began to blend into one
giant Greek salad. This widespread

culture was called Hellenism, after *Hellas*, the Greek word for Greece.

In Judea, a small and poor strip of land that linked Asia and Africa, the Jews weren't entirely happy about the spread of Hellenism. While they appreciated many of the benefits that the Greeks had brought, there were some things that they could not accept. The Jews wouldn't give up their ancient rituals and they refused to bow down to the idols of the Greeks.

To the Hellenistic leaders of Judea, the Jews were a peculiar and stubborn people, but they paid their taxes and they seemed harmless enough. They were allowed to go about their business and worship their nameless, faceless God. They were allowed their holy temple and their holy city of Jerusalem. They were allowed to study the Torah and to live as their ancestors had always lived.

But then, in the year 175 B.C.E. (Before the Common Era), a new dynasty came to power. In its throne sat the Syrian monarch Antiochus Epiphanes, known as Antiochus IV. He wanted everyone under his rule to be Greek in every way. If they refused, they would be killed. Though some Jews gave in, others didn't, and many died for their beliefs.

For months, the people of the Judean village of Modi'in had been talking about the problems the Greeks were causing. Jews in neighboring towns were being coerced to blaspheme by eating unkosher animals, or forced to convert—or die. Much blood was spilled; the old ways were being forgotten. The Jewish people were in danger of being wiped out entirely.

One day a traveler passed
through and spoke to Mattathias,
an old Jewish priest who lived
in Modi'in with his sons, about
a recent happening in Jerusalem.
Elazar, a priest like Mattathias,
had refused to sacrifice a pig for
the honor of the king. The king
tried to strike a deal with Elazar,
offering him his life in exchange
for telling his people that he had
eaten pork. Elazar again refused

and was beaten to death at the age of ninety. This news deeply troubled Mattathias.

Soon, the once great city of Jerusalem became a haven for thieves and killers; its most holy temple became a shrine to the Greek god Zeus. Its altar was defiled with sacrifices of unholy animals. This place that once held such joy for the Jews was now defiled and lost. The Jewish residents of Jerusalem had all fled. The glory of that city was no more. There seemed no end to the troubles caused by Antiochus. Mattathias knew that it was only a matter of time before his soldiers paid Modi'in a visit. What would he and the villagers do then?

Mattathias Is Tested

In 167 B.C.E., the dreaded day arrived when the forces of King Antiochus rode into Modi'in. An officer approached Mattathias at a public gathering and said to him, "You are a leader of your people and the father of five fine sons. Be the first to follow the king's commands and others will follow you."

"What is it you ask of me and of my people?" asked Mattathias.

"We ask only a sacrifice to the glory of the gods and the glory of Antiochus, who is like a god.

Others of your people have offered
similar sacrifices and have been
rewarded with wealth and honor.
You'll be granted these things,
too, if you offer up a pig upon
the altar."

"To do what you ask would be
to forsake my religion and my
ancestors. I would be turning my
back on God himself. I can never
do this thing," swore Mattathias,
seething with rage.

No sooner had Mattathias finished speaking than one of the townspeople of Modi'in, a Jew, brought forward a pig for sacrifice.

When Mattathias saw this blasphemy, he could no longer control his fury. He slew the man right there on the altar. Then he killed the king's officer who was forcing them to sacrifice.

Everyone was stunned.

Mattathias knew that now was

the time for action. He shouted
in a voice loud and strong, "Everyone who is zealous for the law and
supports the covenant with God
come out with me!"

And he and his sons and many
of their friends fled to the hills,
leaving behind all they had.

Others ran off to seek shelter
in the wilderness below. They hid
there, planning what to do next.
Meanwhile, the king's forces rallied.

The townsfolk of Modi'in were now considered rebels and outlaws.

"Come out from where you're hiding," urged the soldiers. "Do what the king commands, and you will live."

But the townsfolk kept silent so as not to reveal their hiding places. It was Sabbath and they had agreed that they would not fight the soldiers, even if attacked. "Let us all die innocent, and heaven and earth will testify that we are killed unjustly."

The soldiers hunted them down like wild animals and killed them all—including women and children.

When news of this horror spread, many Jews felt they had no choice but to convert to the pagan religion. But not everyone—some took action, and their action changed history. The tide would soon turn against King Antiochus.

The Maccabees at War

When Mattathias and his friends in the mountains learned how the army of Antiochus had senselessly slaughtered innocent people, it hardened their resolve. They knew they had no choice but to fight. They organized an army, and soon Jews from other towns who were fleeing the Greeks came and joined them. The Jews learned to be great warriors, even though their numbers were small. They swept into towns to tear down altars set up by the Greeks for their idol worship.

Years went by, and Mattathias grew old. Though there were many skirmishes, the great battle to regain the temple in Jerusalem and make it holy again was yet to be fought. The temple is a symbol of the Jews' right to worship freely. Before Mattathias died he appointed his third son, Judah, to command the army and deliver the Jews to victory.

Judah was a smart, tough man who was unafraid to use force. He became known as Maccabee, which means "the hammer." The civilian army he trained called themselves Maccabees. The Syrians would soon learn that this rag-tag

army of teachers and farmers and weavers was a force to contend with.

What the Maccabees lacked in numbers and strength, they made up in cunning and motivation. The Syrian army fought for cash or because the king commanded them to. Maccabees fought for their God, their beliefs, and their freedom to worship.

Judah Maccabee was a master of guerilla warfare. He and his men would swoop down under cover of night and set fire to the camps of enemy soldiers. No one knew when or where he'd attack. Judah knew all the caves and rock outcrops where he and his troops could hide. He knew where to place himself for the best vantage point, and which mountain passes the Syrians would likely choose. His knowledge of the land made it easy for him to move at a moment's

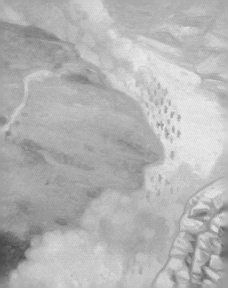

notice and strike seemingly from out of nowhere. He began to be taken seriously.

Soon, he became such a threat that armies were organized against him. His first battle was against General Appolonius, who underestimated the Maccabee forces. The makeshift army beat Appolonius badly, and the general's forces turned tail and fled. That day, the Maccabees gathered up the armor

and weapons of the defeated army
to use as their own. Judah had man-
aged to kill Appolonius. He took
the general's sword and used it for
the rest of his life.

Hearing about the defeat of
Appolonius, General Seron of the
Syrian army thought he would be
able to defeat the Maccabees and
win honor for himself. His army was
twice the size of Appolonius's. He,
too, underestimated his opponent.

Seron's army had to move through a small pass in the mountains in order to get to Judah's men. But Judah's small group was ready for him–they got to the pass first, and when the army approached, the Maccabees were ready with sword in hand. They killed eight hundred of Seron's men. The rest fled. Victory, again, went to the Maccabees.

And on it went. With each victory, more people came to join the cause of the Maccabees. Their ranks swelled, but never approached the numbers of the men who swore to stop them. Judah's success lay not with strength, but with strategy. He had men hiding everywhere, spying on their enemies and ready to report back what they heard so the Maccabees could plan with foresight.

For three difficult years the Maccabees fought, finally making their way into Jerusalem to reclaim the Holy Temple. And when they arrived there, they faced what might have been their hardest work of all—cleaning it up and making it holy once again.

Rededication of the Holy Temple

One of the Jews' most sacred places lay in ruins. The altar had been destroyed, and unclean animals had been sacrificed upon the place where it once stood. Statues of Greek gods ruled over the cluttered mess. All that was beautiful or useful had been broken or stolen. When the Jews saw this they wept and prayed. Then they went to work.

They swept out the filth and the shards of shattered pottery. They pushed out the statues. They tore down the crumbled, polluted altar and built a clean, new one out of whole stones, according to ancient law. Potters and metal-workers busied themselves making candlesticks, incense burners, and pots for sacred oil. Young children

helped pull weeds and plant flow-
ers in the outside courtyard. Walls
and floors were scrubbed inside
and out. Old women sewed cur-
tains to adorn the windows. The
smell of fresh bread perfumed the
air and drove out the mustiness.

Finally, on the twenty-fifth day
of the third month of the Jewish
calendar, the month known as
Kislev, the temple was ready. The
year was 164 B.C.E. The Macca-

bees dedicated the temple, offering a sacrifice to God. The celebration was to last eight glorious days. There was only one problem—a celebration as important as this required the purest oil for its candelabra. Most of the oil in the temple had been tainted. The Maccabees found just one sealed flask that was worthy of use—with enough to last but a single day. One flask would have to do.

And, miraculously, it did! The dedication festivities went on without interruption as the oil burned for more than a week. This was a small but significant miracle that illuminated the greater miracle of the Maccabees' victory over their enemies. What's perhaps the greatest miracle of all is that those lights are still burning just as bright today as we celebrate Hanukkah in our own homes. The word Hanukkah has come to mean "dedication"–not just the dedication of the Holy Temple, but also the dedication it took the Maccabees to persevere in very dangerous and difficult times.

Celebration

Games,
Recipes,
and Songs

The word "dreidel" is
Yiddish for top.
The Hebrew word is *sivivon*.

Some believe that the dreidel's
ancestor is a toy top
with which German boys
and girls played.

One legend traces the dreidel back to the time of the Maccabees (167 B.C.E.). To escape King Antiochus's spies, who were always on the lookout for Jews gathering to study the Torah—an activity forbidden by the King—a dreidel was always kept nearby.

If a soldier was approaching, someone would grab the dreidel and spin it. As far as Antiochus's lackeys knew, the Jews had only come together to play a harmless game.

Each side of the dreidel has a Hebrew
letter. Each letter represents the
first letter of each word in the
sentence *Nais gadol hayah sham*, which
means "A great miracle happened
there." (That miracle, of course,
is the recapture of the Holy Temple
of Jerusalem by the Maccabees.)

Celebration

In Israel, dreidels are a little different. They follow the sentence, *Nais gadol hayah poh*, or "**A** great miracle happened here," because Israel is where the miracle happened.

Celebration

The letters on the dreidel have come to stand for other words, which form the basis of the dreidel game. In Yiddish, נ (*nun*) stands for *nicht*, which means "take nothing;" ג (*gimel*) stands for *ganz*, or "take all;" ה (*heh*) represents *halb* or "take half;" and ש (*shin*) means *shtell*, or "put in."

You can play the dreidel game
with whatever you'd like, but
many people play with pennies.
To play, divide the pennies
equally between the players.
Each player puts a penny in the
pot, and then the first player
takes a turn at spinning the
dreidel. If the dreidel lands on
ה (heh), the player takes
half the pot. If the dreidel falls

on 𝁇 (shin), the first player
gives half her pile to the pot. If
it lands on 𝁂 (gimel), she gets to
take all the pennies in the pot.
If the dreidel lands on 𝁃 (nun),
nothing happens. Each
player then puts another penny
in the pot, and the second
player spins the dreidel.
The game continues until one
person wins all the pennies.

on שׁ (shin), the first player gives half her pile to the pot. If it lands on ג (gimel), she gets to take all the pennies in the pot. If the dreidel lands on נ (nun), nothing happens. Each player then puts another penny in the pot, and the second player spins the dreidel. The game continues until one person wins all the pennies.

Hanukkah is a time of great feasting and merriment. Because of the holiday's connection with miraculous oil, Hanukkah foods are traditionally fried.

Celebration

Our family tradition has always
included baking lots of
Hanukkah cookies. We had
a special set of cookie cutters
that formed perfect stars,
dreidels, and [menorahs].
Sometimes we just made round
cookies and frosted them
with blue and white icing.

Judy Zeidler
Jewish chef

For American Jews intrigued with the gastronomic side of Judaism, Hanukkah appears to be the preferred holiday. It is difficult to equal the taste of brown, crisp potato latkes. Can gefilte fish, matzoh balls, haroset, or even hamantashen compare with them? Certainly not.

Joan Nathan
American chef

HAROSET

GEFILTE · FISH

MATZOH · BALLS

HAMANTASHEN

LATKES

During Hanukkah,
the oil knows
no miracles . . . we
use two or three
bottles that week.

Arlene Rossen Cardozo
American writer

Celebration

Hanukkah smells like latkes.

Malka Drucker
American writer

**Hanukkah latkes teach
us that man cannot
live by miracles alone.**

Proverb

Latkes

Ingredients:

5 medium potatoes

1 medium onion

1 egg

1 teaspoon salt

a dash of pepper

2 tablespoons flour or matzoh meal

oil for frying

1. Peel the potatoes and onions, then grate them. The coarse

side of the grater will make the latkes more crunchy; the fine side will make them creamier.

2. Add the egg, salt, pepper, and flour or matzoh meal. Mix well.

3. Pour enough oil into a skillet to cover the bottom generously.

4. Heat the pan over medium. You'll know it's hot enough when a pinch of flour sizzles. Don't let the oil get so hot that it smokes.

5. Spoon the batter into the pan. The pancakes should be 3-4 inches across.
6. Fry until brown on one side, then flip them and brown the other side.
7. Carefully lift the latkes out and drain them on paper towels.
8. Serve 'em up! Try them with apple sauce or grated cheese.

Other traditions are dairy foods and candies made of sesame seeds, fruits, and nuts. Eastern European Jewish families use kasha, a form of buckwheat, in many forms during Hanukkah, including blintzes, kreplach, and kasha varnishkes.

Judy Zeidler
Jewish chef

On the last day of Hanukkah,
some Turkish Jews enjoy
a special meal called *merenda*,
at which many relatives and
friends gather, each bringing
a portion of the food to be
shared by everyone present.

Gloria Kaufer Greene
American editor

Different communities have
different customs.
Ashkenazic Jews often make
potato latkes fried in oil.
Sephardic Jews specialize in
jam-filled doughnuts.

Dr. Shmuel Himelstein
American editor

SOOFGANIYOT

PONCHIKS

Yeast Doughnuts

Ingredients:

2 cups flour

2 teaspoons baking powder

$1/2$ teaspoon cinnamon

pinch salt

1 egg

$1/2$ cup sugar

$1/2$ cup milk

2 tablespoons melted butter or margarine

Oil for deep frying

Powdered sugar for sprinkling

1. In a large bowl, mix together the flour, baking powder, cinnamon, and salt. Set aside.
2. In another bowl, beat the egg. Then slowly add the sugar, beating constantly.
3. Add the milk and melted butter to the egg mixture.
4. Pour the wet ingredients into the dry ingredients. Mix well. This is your dough.
5. Roll the dough out onto a lightly

floured board to a thickness
of about a half an inch. Use
the rim of a glass to mark two-
or three-inch diameter circles.
To make a smaller circle, use
the lid or neck of a soda bottle.
Use a knife to cut out the center
of the circles. (You can fry these
cut-outs separately, or re-roll
them into more doughnuts.)

6. In a heavy, deep pot, heat
   four or five inches of oil over

medium heat. You'll know it's ready when a pinch of the dough sizzles and browns quickly. If the oil smokes, it's too hot.

7. Put the doughnuts in the oil a few at a time. Don't crowd them or they won't cook fast enough and they'll be greasy. They should take two to three minutes per side to reach a nice golden color.

8. As they come out, drain them on paper towels.

9. Sprinkle with powdered sugar just before serving.

Ma'oz Tzur (Rock of Ages)
was composed in
Europe by a man named
Mordechai, sometime
in the twelfth or
thirteenth century.
Little is known about him.

Ma'oz Tzur

(Rock of Ages)

Ma'oz Tzur y'shu-a-ti
L'kha na-eh lisha-bay-akh
Ti-kon beit t-fila-ti
V'sham to-da n'za-bay-akh
L-eit takhin mat-bay-akh
Mitzar ham'na-bay-akh
Az egmor b-shir miz-mor
chanukat hamiz-bay-akh

Rock of Ages, let our song
praise Thy saving power.
Thou amidst our raging foes
were our sheltering tower.
Furious they assailed us
when Thine arm availed us.
And Thy word broke their
  sword
when our own strength
  failed us.

Mi Y'maleil

(Who Can Retell?)

Mi y'ma-lel g'vu-rot Yisrael?
O tan-mi yim-ne?
Hen b'hol dor ya-kum ha-ge-bor
go el ha-em.
Sh'ma!

Ba-yam ha-heim baz'man
   ha-zeh

125

Maccabi moshiya u-fodeh
Uv'yameinu kol a Yisrael
Yit'ached yakum l'hi-ga-el

Who can retell the things
     that befell them?
Who can count them?
In every age a hero or sage
     arose to our aid.

Celebration

Hark!
In days of old in Israel's
ancient land
Brave Maccabeus led his
faithful band.
But now all Israel must as
one arise,
Redeem itself through deed
and sacrifice.

This book has been bound using handcraft methods and Smyth-sewn to ensure durability.

The dust jacket and interior were illustrated by Marco Ventura and designed by Corinda Cook.

The stories were retold by Steven Zorn.

The text was edited by Caroline Tiger and Melissa Wagner.

The text was set in Matura, Gill Sans, and Caslon.